STICKER STORIES

In the GARDEN

Walter Foster Jr.

Illustrated by Nila Aye

Written by Samantha Chagollan

Printed in China
1 3 5 7 9 10 8 6 4 2

FSC
www.fsc.org
MIX
Paper from
responsible sources
FSC® C016973

How to Use This Book

It's easy to create your own stories
with stickers and drawings of your
garden friends!

Here's what
you need:

- This book
- Blank drawing paper
- Pencils, an eraser,
  and crayons
- Your imagination!

Eraser

Here's what you do:

1 *Make a Scene*
Fill up the story pages with stickers to complete the scenes.

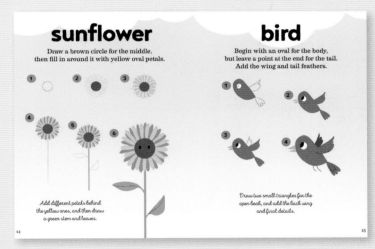

2 *Draw It Out*
Follow the simple steps to draw your own characters.

3 *Tell a Story*
Combine stickers and drawings to make your own adventures, starting with the scene on page 24!

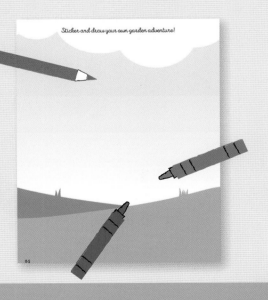

What will the bunny find to nibble on in the garden?

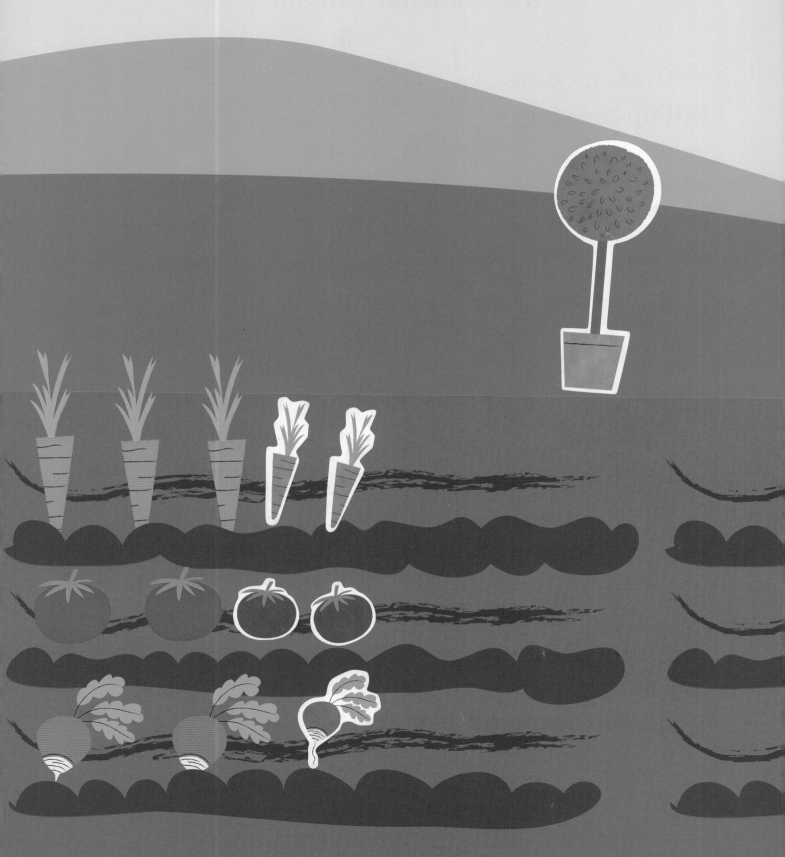

Add stickers to show what is growing in the soil!
Who else is playing in the garden?

rabbit

Draw an oval for the head,
and a long, thin rectangle for the body.

Add the front and
back legs, and two
long, floppy ears.
Hippity hop!

carrot

Draw a long, skinny triangle,
pointing down.

Then add the
greenery and detail
lines to finish.

Piper the dog loves to chase squirrels. What else will he find in the orchard today?

Add stickers to show what else is growing in the orchard!

tree

Draw the fluffy, curvy lines of the tree's leaves. Then add the trunk with a rectangle.

Add some branches and some roots too. Finally, add the details to make it look real!

squirrel

Start by drawing the squirrel's head, and then add the body, legs, and arms.

Draw a big, bushy tail and give her a little acorn to munch on!

The scarecrow is looking after the field today.
What is growing in the field?

sunflower

Draw a brown circle for the middle,
then fill in around it with yellow oval petals.

1

2

3

4

5

6

*Add different petals behind
the yellow ones, and then draw
a green stem and leaves.*

bird

Begin with an oval for the body,
but leave a point at the end for the tail.
Add the wing and tail feathers.

*Draw two small triangles for the
open beak, and add the back wing
and final details.*

Edwin the gnome needs help planting his garden. Who has come to help?

Add stickers of flowers
and friends in Edwin's garden.

mushroom

A half-circle makes the top of the mushroom, and a curvy rectangle shape makes the stem.

1

2

3

Add some big, fun dots to the top of the mushroom, and a wavy line to the stem.

4

snail

This snail's shell is a circle. Fill in the shell, and then add the snail's head and tail.

Don't forget to draw the antennae and the spiral on the shell!

What a beautiful morning in the garden!
Look at all the beautiful flowers!

Who has come to smell the flowers?
Add some stickers of bees and bugs!

grasshopper

Draw a circle for the head and a half-circle for the body. Then draw the legs.

Add the final details, and this little green guy is ready to hop away!

dragonfly

Once you have drawn a circle for the head, add another for the body.

Then add a long, skinny oval for the tail, four light blue wings, and all the details.

Sticker and draw your own garden adventure!